Made in the USA
Monee, IL
09 February 2022

90961592R00061